NEW YORK CITY
THE FIVE BOROUGHS

A PICTORIAL SOUVENIR

CAROL M. HIGHSMITH AND TED LANDPHAIR

NEW YORK CITY
THE FIVE BOROUGHS
A PICTORIAL SOUVENIR

CRESCENT BOOKS

NEW YORK

THE AUTHORS GRATEFULLY ACKNOWLEDGE
THE SERVICES, ACCOMMODATIONS, AND SUPPORT PROVIDED BY
HILTON HOTELS CORPORATION
AND THE
FORT LEE HILTON, FORT LEE, NEW JERSEY
IN CONNECTION WITH THE COMPLETION OF THIS BOOK.

———

This 1997 edition is published by Crescent Books,
a division of Random House Value Publishing, Inc.,
201 East 50th Street, New York, N.Y. 10022.

Crescent Books and colophon are trademarks of
Random House Value Publishing, Inc.

Random House
New York • Toronto • London • Sydney • Auckland
http://www.randomhouse.com/

Printed and bound in China

A CIP catalog record for this book is available from
the Library of Congress

ISBN 0-517-20147-X

8   7   6   5   4   3   2   1

———

Designed by Robert L. Wiser, Archetype Press, Inc., Washington, D.C.

PAGES 2–3: *The Manhattan skyline, viewed from Ellis Island, looked nothing like this when most European immigrants arrived at the processing center in the years straddling the turn of the century. Although the city got its first modest high-rise in 1887, it was not until the 1930s that eye-popping skyscrapers like the Empire State and Chrysler buildings began to crowd into hundreds of blocks of Midtown. Completed in 1977, the twin 110-story towers of the World Trade Center now dominate the skyline.*

FOREWORD

To many, New York City, that colossus of roads, bridges, skyscrapers, and humanity, *is* America. From its pastoral beginnings, this city grew to encompass dozy villages and working farms, urban grandeur and surburban sprawl. Indeed, New York—big, boastful, materialistic, and multicultural since its inception—anticipated the America of today.

From the beginning, New York City was a business venture. And when Brooklyn, Staten Island, the Bronx, and Queens were added, in the 1890's, to the borough of Manhattan, creating Greater New York, 650 miles of oceanfront land became available for development and commerce. New York was thus ideally situated to dominate trade with both Europe and the American continent.

Greater New York has a striking collective personality, yet each of its five boroughs retains a unique character of its own. Manhattan, often defined by its famous skyscrapers, most notably the Empire State and Chrysler buildings and the World Trade Center's twin towers, also possesses the magnificent 843-acre Central Park. Manhattan's fabled "Museum Mile" on Fifth Avenue, boasts an array of legendary cultural institutions, including the Metropolitan Museum of Art and The Guggenheim Museum. An architectural and cultural treasure trove of great buildings, churches, and institutions, from Wall Street to Harlem, Soho to Times Square, the East Village to the Upper West Side, Manhattan's neighborhoods themselves have become popular tourist spots.

Brooklyn, the city's most nostalgic borough, conjures up images of the Dodgers playing ball at Ebbets Field, of Coney Island's exotic attractions, of pungent "Brookyn accents," and stately brownstone neighborhoods like Cobble Hill, Park Slope, and Brooklyn Heights. Some of the borough's many cultural landmarks include The Brooklyn Museum, enormous Green-Wood Cemetery, "Brooklyn's Garden City of the Dead," and Prospect Park. Two of New York's finest cultural fixtures, The Bronx Zoo and the New York Botanical Garden, thrive in New York's northern borough, the Bronx, home of the world champion Yankees. The first four houses of the Historic House Trust of New York, including the home where Edgar Allen Poe wrote some of his greatest works, are also found in the Bronx. Admirers of Queens, the largest and most residential borough, speak of the neighborhood identities that have lingered. Alongside the close-knit communities of Astoria, Jackson Heights, and Floral Park, amongst others, can be found such amenities as the Socrates Sculpture Park. And Staten Island, the last of the boroughs to be connected by bridge with another, remains proud of its world-famous ferry, its independent air, and its Historic Richmond Town. A lively arts and humanities council presents free concerts and performances, several times a month, all across the island from which, thanks to its hilly terrain, some of the best views of the Brooklyn and Manhattan skylines can be seen.

A brave, brash, ultimately great city, New York, in all its protean energy and strength, continues to stimulate, challenge, and reward all who experience it—immigrants, residents, and visitors alike.

Ellis Island's processing center (opposite) replaced a wooden structure destroyed by fire. The Golden Door to a new life for seventeen million Americans was abandoned to the salt air and vandals after World War II until the most ambitious restoration project in American history in the 1980s refurbished it and the Statue of Liberty. Restorers were amazed to find that of twenty-eight thousand ceiling tiles inside Ellis Island's main building (above), only seventeen required replacing. Once they were cleared to enter the United States, many immigrants proceeded to Manhattan's southernmost tip at Battery Park (overleaf). Today it's the terminus of the Staten Island Ferry as well as a hot residential neighborhood on ninety-two reclaimed acres, below Lower Manhattan's bustling financial district. Site of the first Dutch settlement of New Amsterdam, Battery Park took its name from British cannons arrayed there in the early 1600s.

Arturo DiModica's bronze Charging Bull *(above)*, sculpted in 1987 after a pro-longed dip in stock prices, has become a symbol of optimism on New York's Wall Street. Trowbridge & Livingston added a neoclassical pediment to the New York Stock Exchange Building *(right)* in 1923. The building was elaborately designed in 1901, at the height of the nation's optimism. OPPOSITE: Inside, visitors can take a self-guided tour and peer down on the trading floor, which is less chaotic than it used to be, thanks to extensive electronic trading. The exchange was first created to handle $80 million in U.S. bonds used to pay Revolutionary War debts.

NYSE
The world puts its stock in us.
its stock in us.
5
10

New York's most famous church, Saint Patrick's Cathedral, named for the patron saint of Ireland and home to the wealthiest Roman Catholic archdiocese in the United States, is the scene of many high-society weddings. Consecrated in 1879 but not completed until 1906, it is the shrine of the nation's first male saint, Saint John Neumann. Inside architect James Renwick Jr.'s French Gothic creation, the great baldachin, or canopy, above the high altar (opposite) is made of bronze. Its ornate, 330-foot twin spires (left) stand in marked contrast to stolid Rockefeller Center across the street, and the shiny, black-glass Olympic Tower to the rear. For decades, until the age of skyscrapers, the spires— which were finished in 1888—dominated the midtown skyline.

Stone sentry lions guard the entrance to the New York Public Library's main building, an artistic and intellectual treasure. It was established by combining a number of private collections, including that of John Jacob Astor. The Beaux Arts structure, designed by Carrère & Hastings, cost the city $9 million when it opened in 1911. RIGHT: Henry Hardenbergh designed the landmark Plaza Hotel, overlooking Central Park off Fifth Avenue. Its rounded corner tower was the epitome of French Renaissance styling popular at the time. OPPOSITE: Jules-Alexis Coutans's sculpture of Mercury, Hercules, and Minerva was carefully refurbished during a meticulous restoration of the 1913 Grand Central Terminal in the early 1990s.

ND CENTRAL
MINAL

OPPOSITE: *Even the Chrysler Building's gargoyles are stainless steel. William Van Alen's seventy-seven-story Art Deco jewel typified the race to be the world's tallest building. Its shining spire was hidden in the fire shaft until the unveiling, then dramatically raised to give it supremacy. More than sixteen thousand people work in the massive Art Deco Empire State Building (left), which immodestly calls itself the "Eighth Wonder of the World."* ABOVE: *Rockefeller Center occupies twenty-two acres of prime mid-town property. The sprawling complex, whose construction began during the Great Depression, includes nineteen entertainment, shopping, and office buildings. The towering General Electric Building is its hub.*

The Secretariat Building is the most recognizable landmark within the United Nations complex (above), designed by an international committee led by American Wallace Harrison. Flags of member nations ring the plaza outside, and artwork of dozens of nations abounds inside. General Assembly sessions are open to the public on a first-come, first-admitted basis. RIGHT: Park Avenue is lined with posh hotels, private palaces, and elegant apartment buildings designed by New York's top architects. Many great mansions are now international consulates, missions, and cultural institutes. Others were donated by their wealthy owners for use by charitable and other not-for-profit agencies.

Architect Calvert Vaux and landscape architect Frederick Law Olmsted collaborated on the design of New York's "backyard"—Central Park, which replaced miserable bogs and squatters' shacks and is, by law, forever protected from development. Figures from Hans Christian Andersen to Alice in Wonderland are remembered with statues in the park. Yoko Ono paid to have a section restored as the international Strawberry Fields peace garden in memory of her slain husband, John Lennon. Paul Manship's 1932 bronze Group of Bears (above) stands just inside Central Park.

E AMERICAN MVSEVM OF NATVRAL HISTORY
FOVNDED 1869

Several famous architects, including Calvert Vaux and John Russell Pope, had a hand in the design and expansions of the American Museum of Natural History (left). Its more than thirty-six million artifacts include meteor fragments, lifelike dioramas, and a huge dinosaur collection. ABOVE: *The memorial to Union general Ulysses Grant, popularly known as "Grant's Tomb," also holds the remains of the general's wife.*

John Duncan's white-granite mausoleum is modeled after Napoleon's final resting place, Les Invalides in Paris. Bronze busts in the crypt depict Grant's subordinates. Inside the Cloisters (overleaf), the Metropolitan Museum of Art's medieval-style annex in Fort Tryon Park, a fifteenth-century Spanish tempera and oil triptych hangs above a German altarpiece, c. 1470, and busts of female saints.

ALLEVA
OVER 100 YEARS
Ricotta ALLEVA Mozzarella
RICOTTA · ALLEVA · MOZZARELLA 188
Alleva
BEST QUALITY
Alleva
BEST QUALITY
ITALIAN SPECIALTIES
PROSCIUTTO SOPRESSATA CAPICOLLO
Piemonte Ravi
190 FRESH PASTA MADE HERE
PIEMONTE
RAVIOLI CO.
OPEN
PIEMONTE
RAVIOLI CO.

The size of Little Italy (opposite) has shrunk as Chinatown expands. Savory holdouts, including restaurants, cheese shops, and delicatessens, can be found along Mulberry Street. In Greenwich Village, even the firehouses (top left) are charming. Cheap rents attracted writers like Walt Whitman and artists like John La Farge. The Access NYC guide calls the Village "the birthplace of the bohemian spirit." BOTTOM: M. Chemiakin's 1993 bronze Cybele: Goddess of Fertility is a prominent fixture at Mimi Ferzt's gallery in artsy SoHo.

Restaurant
Sylvia's
RESTAURANT
SOUL FOOD
Sylvia's

Sylvia's Restaurant (opposite), named for Sylvia Woods, the "Queen of Soul Food," is patronized as much by tourists as by locals. The new Cotton Club nightclub (left) replaced a Harlem entertainment institution where downtown whites pulled up in limousines to hear Duke Ellington, Cab Calloway, and other legendary musicians. The club's replacement still features blues and jazz on "Harlem's Main Street" under the entryway to the George Washington Bridge.

Yankee Stadium in the Bronx (preceding pages) is the "House that [Babe] Ruth Built"—and owner George Steinbrenner renovated. The fortunes of the team once called the "Bronx Bombers" seemed to mirror those of the borough: like the Bronx, the Yanks went downhill in the 1980s, only to rebound in the last decade of the century. Just up the hill from Yankee Stadium, a relief sets a heroic tone at the Bronx Courthouse (top right). The Hall of Fame for Great Americans (bottom) at Bronx Community College stands on the highest natural point in New York City. It was dedicated in 1901 as a pantheon honoring historically significant men and women. Pictured is the Scientist and Inventor Wing. OPPOSITE: The upper Bronx holds innumerable surprises, including elegant homes.

The "Rainey Gates" (left) open into the Bronx Zoo (now properly called the International Wildlife Conservation Park), America's largest urban zoo. The gates, erected in 1933 by sculptor Paul Manship in the French Arts Decoratifs style, was dedicated in memory of big-game hunter and zoo patron Paul J. Rainey. ABOVE: Monkeys, tapirs, leopards, and other species live in JungleWorld, a re-created Southeast Asian rain forest, mangrove swamp, and scrub forest. In recent years the zoo, which was founded in 1899, has concentrated on housing vanishing species and perpetuating endangered creatures such as the snow leopard. It operates satellite wildlife centers in Queens, Manhattan's Central Park, and Brooklyn's Prospect Park.

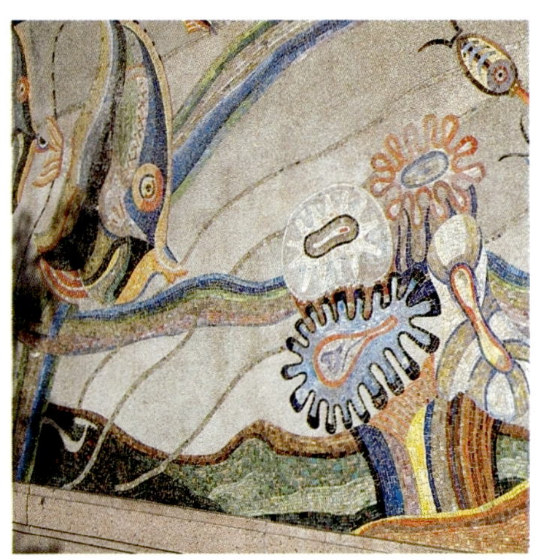

The mosaic above appears on a building along the Bronx's Grand Concourse, designed in 1892 to connect Manhattan with its new "annexed district." Dozens of Art Deco and Art Moderne apartment buildings appeared along the four-mile-long raised "speedway" in the 1930s. Several winning entries in the America's Cup sailing races were built in boathouses on City Island (right), the Bronx's taste of New England on Long Island Sound. The island is wildly eclectic: next door to the weathered North Wind Undersea Institute Museum is an old sea captain's home that has been turned into Le Refuge Bed & Breakfast, run by Pierre Saint-Denis, one of Manhattan's renowned chefs. OVERLEAF: Queens is one of the few remaining places where the "subway" (overleaf) is still elevated in spots.

7 Main St. Flushing
Exit Manhatt
xit
Off-hour trains

The New York Hall of Science and the Unisphere (opposite), relics of the 1964 World's Fair, can be found in Flushing Meadows Corona Park in Queens. The Hall of Science was the fair's Science Pavilion. Its interactive displays and video screens that can magnify microscopic particles delight visitors. The undulating building, clad in concrete panels studded with stained glass, is itself a curiosity. The 380-ton Unisphere, designed by Peter Muller-Munk, Inc., features a grid representing the earth as well as orbiting satellites. Wading in its reflecting pool is almost de rigeuer for children visiting Corona Park. OVERLEAF: Nearly hidden off Vernon Boulevard along the East River in Queens is the Socrates Sculpture Park, a seemingly haphazard collection of sculptures that frame the Manhattan skyline most unusually. Fodor's guide says its abstract artwork "first appears almost as an urban hallucination."

ATHENA'S
Nails

The boroughs outside Manhattan are full of ethnic surprises. Greek restaurants, grocery stores, and shops like this nail salon (opposite) abound in the Astoria section of Queens. Authentic Italian markets (top left) tempt the taste buds along Arthur Avenue in the Belmont-Arthur section of the Bronx. Parts of Main Street in Flushing, Queens, have become virtual Asian bazaars (bottom), where vendors serve delicacies like Chinese steamed dumplings. OVERLEAF: Hidden among Brooklyn's tall buildings, as seen from South Street Seaport in Manhattan, are many ethnic culinary and fashion delights, an easy subway ride away. Brooklyn's Cobble Hill neighborhood, for instance, is crammed with Italian restaurants and shops, which fill Court Street with the intoxicating smells of pasta, cheeses, olives, and sauces.

TO THE DEFENDERS OF THE UNION 1861 1865

*Grand Army Plaza
(page 50) in
Brooklyn's Park Slope
is anchored by the
Soldiers' and Sailors'
Memorial Arch,
inspired by the Arc
de Triomphe in Paris.
Frederick McMonnies
created the heroic
four-horse chariot.
Richard Upjohn
designed the ornate
Gothic gateway to
Brooklyn's Green-
Wood Cemetery (page
51), where many
New York notables—
Samuel F. B. Morse,
Nathaniel Currier,
and James Ives,
among them—
found eternal rest.
The New York Transit
Museum (above),
in an abandoned
Brooklyn station,
offers plenty of
chances to catch an
informative "ride."
McKim, Mead &
White designed the
Brooklyn Museum
building (right) in
1897. The museum's
African and pre-
Columbian collections
are world-renowned.*

CONVERGING CULTURES
SOLON
PINDAR
AESCHYLVS
ROOKLYN MUSEUM

WONDER WHEEL
Denos SWEET SHOPPE
cotton candy · popcorn · candy apples · churros · funnel cake
Tickets

Brooklyn's Coney Island (left), the "World's Largest Playground," first drew fun-seekers from throughout the boroughs because of its unbeatable one-two punch: a rollicking amusement park and fine Atlantic Ocean beaches. Some say Coney Island hot dogs alone are still worth a visit. The subway's arrival in 1920, soon followed by completion of the park's boardwalk, sealed its popularity, which withstood the Depression, deterioration of the old wooden roller coasters, and construction of public housing just across the road. Next door is New York's Aquarium (above), a branch of the Wildlife Conservation Society. Its Conservation Hall features colorful exhibits from the Belize Coral Reefs, the Amazon River, and the depths of several oceans.

Staten Is

Staten Islanders were happy with their ferry (left), though not always with the frequency of service. There was little groundswell for a bridge to other boroughs, but one was built anyway. The Verrazano-Narrows Bridge brought tens of thousands of new residents, mostly from Brooklyn, to which it connected, and also development that quickened the pace of life on the previously drowsy island. One link to the past, however, is Historic Richmond Town— twenty-seven authentic and historic buildings, including the remark- ably restored 1837 Stephens's General Store (overleaf). Richmond Town was the bustling seat of the original county of that name that comprised Staten Island. Special programs on the area's history, agri- culture, commerce, and maritime life are offered year-round there.

NIAGARA BAKERY
CRACKERS & BISCUITS
GOLD COIN

FRENCH'S PURE SPICES
ABSOLUTELY PURE
CANDIES
Holmes & Coutts BISCUITS
ENG. BREAKFAST
No. 1

Some of Staten Island's large Roman Catholic population has been served since 1919 by Saint Peter's Church, a detail of which is shown above. Somehow, the sanctuary, rectory, and bell tower all manage to hug a steep cliff overlooking Richmond Terrace in Saint George. Carefully restored houses like this one in Tottenville (right) can be found throughout Staten Island. The home was built in 1892 by John Brown's shipyard workers as a wedding gift to Brown and his bride. OVERLEAF: In the Livingston neighborhood, the old Sailors Snug Harbor— a maritime hospital and home for retired sailors—has been converted into serene Snug Harbor, which includes acres of parkland, fountains, and performance halls.